ENGAGE
Totally Simple Bible Studies for Teen Girls
moretobe.com

Journey to Freedom

A STUDY ABOUT IDENTITY

LEADER'S GUIDE

Elisa Pulliam
moretobe.com

Dedication

Especially for the girls next door
and across the field,
who remind me how this
generation is longing for answers.

Table of Contents

How this Works

Titus 2:4-5 NLT

These older women must train the younger women to love their husbands and their children,
to live wisely and be pure, to work in their homes, to do good, and to be submissive to their husbands.
Then they will not bring shame on the word of God.

"It wasn't what I expected."

That pretty much sums up how I've responded to every single mentoring gathering I've led over the last five years. Even though I have girls in my home nearly every month, I always fall into the trap of believeing that I should be prepared for whatever may happen. Isn't there some measure of predicatability? Oh no!

> **I can never guarantee how many girls will show up. . . or how few.**

> **I will never know how many questions will be asked. . . or which ones I'll feel good about answering.**

> **I can't predict how deep the girls will go with their scribbled-on-index-cards curiousities.**

> **I won't be able to know if they'll be a quiet bunch. . . or eager to hear more stories.**

> **I won't ever know if their darting eyes are a sign of pricked hearts. . . or distracted thoughts about what's happening in their lives behind the scenes.**

I really never know what to expect.

And, let me just say that you will likely never know either.

The trouble with putting yourself out there as a leader and being willing to sacrifice your time to mentor teen girls (even one girl, who may very well be your own daughter), is that the return may not be quantifiable or noticeable. . . .ever.

So let me ask you, are you still willing to move forward, if the only one you're really serving and pleasing is God?

Nearly twenty years ago, I got together with two of my dear friends and decided to host a Bible Study on Saturday afternoons for a group of teenage girls. Oh, to our delight when more than a dozen signed up and seemed eagerly committed to give up their free time to dig into the Word with us. The first week, nearly all the girls showed up. We were estatic! The second week, a few dropped out. By the third week, there were only two girls left. And the following week, none came. None. NONE! We sat there, these three 20-somethings passionate about impacting the next generation, with no one to impact. We prayed and asked God to show us what to do differently — and asked Him to even bring the girls back to us.

They never came!

No one ever showed. Not that day and not the next week or the week after. Of course we were discouraged, but we also saw God's purposes at work. The three of us grew closer to each other and spent time preparing for the study in ways we might not have done without the accountability of hosting the study. While this investment of our time might have been considered a waste, our purposes to impact the next generation were playing out in a different way. *God's way.* See, He was simply using our plan to redirect us into His purposes — to grow us in our faith and prepare us for future leading and learning opportunities.

Preparing Thy Self

Since you picked up this study, I'm sure you have a passion to impact the next generation! I'm confident that the Lord is already equipping you for the journey! But I also know the girls you think should show up might very well stand you up. It's quite possible that the Truth you hope to impart on them may be redirected by the Holy Spirit in an unexpected way. You may even find yourself in a difficult situation, or two, where you'll need to depend on the other women involved to carry out your vision and God's purposes.

I share this reality with you, because I want to encourage you to surrender your plans and dreams for this study to the Lord before you even begin.

> ***I want you to be moldable clay in the Potter's hands,***
> ***and allow Him to do His thing, His way.***

God will make this entire experience eternally beautiful — within you, within them, with those looking on — even if you can't figure out what in the world He is doing! But in order for God to accomplish His purposes, you'll need to make a decision now to not get in His way, nor give up. You'll have to shift your expectations from looking for some measure of earthly significance and results that come from this commitment to focusing on doing it all for the glory of God.

Colossians 3:23 NLT
Work willingly at whatever you do, as though you were working for the Lord rather than for people.

It is my hope and prayer for you to pursue leading this study for the glory of God. For His honor! For His delight! For His purposes!

Ironically, that is really what this study is all about. So as you're imparting identity-truths into the next generation, you'l be challenged to soak them in for yourself. You'll be stretched to receive God's promises that declare your worth — simply because you're His child — while the enemy will be tempting you to believe that your value comes from doing this act of service. On those days when you feel out of sorts, Satan will be right there tormenting you. He'll whisper condemnation into your heart, attempting to convince you that you messed up because you forgot to mention "such and such," overlooked *that* detail, or are nothing but a reject because no one showed up.

Oh yes, in the years I've spent leading girls through this identity topic, God has challenged me to grow, too, especially on my bad days. But the lessons aren't all ugly. Some are sweet and tender, as God has healed my heart and caused me to embrace my identity in Christ on a deeper level. I am certain that God, who loves us all so very much, will plan on transforming you through this process, too — as you serve, lead, and impact the next generation for His glory.

What's Inside?

This study is written especially for teenage girls to use with their mom, mentors, youth leaders, or a Sunday school teacher. When I say teen girl, I use the term loosely. Really, the content would be perfect any girl age 12 and up, regardless of her faith upbringing. If you're working with girls who've been immersed in the culture, this study may fit them as young as age 10. The Gospel message is laid out clearly, without assuming that the participants know Jesus as their personal Savior.

The participant's guide is the girl's version of this study. It includes an introductory chapter, which explains what the study is all about and can be read aloud on the first meeting or in advance. The study includes only four chapters — yes, it is intentionally short! Each chapter includes questions at the end, which are designed to get the girls thinking, praying, and reading Scripture on their own. Ideally, the girls will do the week's reading and answer the questions before meeting for the study. However, you could do the work together and use the questions in their workbook to facilitate discussion and connection. At the end of each section of questions, you'll find a reminder to visit http://www.moretobe.com/freedom-resources for additional resources to enhance the study experience.

In this leader's guide, you'll find additional questions and activity ideas to expand the study experience. The leader's guide follows the same flow as the participant's guide, with additional information on the side margins.

What's the Plan?

There are a number of different ways you can work through the material. My hope is that you'll take these suggestions and make it work for you and your girls.

One-on-One or Group Bible Study

Follow this five week schedule and plan for a two hour study session.

Week 1

- Welcome the girls to your study.
- Offer something sweet to eat and tea!
- Start off with introductions and maybe a game to get to know each other.
- Share your faith-story and why leading this study is important to you.
- Read through introduction together.
- Discuss what you've learned and what you hope to get out of the study.

Week 2

- Offer something sweet to eat and tea!
- Focus on Chapter 1 content and questions.
- Do an activity or two.
- Close in prayer.

Week 3

- Offer something sweet to eat and tea!
- Focus on Chapter 2 content and questions.
- Do an activity or two.
- Close in prayer.

Week 4

- Offer something sweet to eat and tea!
- Focus on Chapter 3 content and questions.
- Do an activity or two.
- Close in prayer.

Week 5

- Offer something sweet to eat and tea!
- Focus on Chapter 4 content and questions.
- Do an activity or two.
- Close in prayer.
- Plan a celebration party for finishing the study!

ETC or Mugs & Mornings Mentoring Group Format

If you would like to make this study less formal, I recommend using the ETC Mentoring Gathering method, which doesn't require a commitment on the part of your participants and can be done in one-hour sessions.

- Plan on hosting a gathering once a month.
- Send out invitations / announcements to the girls a few days in advance.
- Begin the gathering with tea and treats, inviting the girls to grab a seat.
- If there are new girls, do a brief introduction about why you're doing this.
- Let the girls introduce themselves to each other.
- Teach on the topic presented in the chapter, sharing for about 10 minutes.
- Encourage the girls to ask their questions using index cards.
- After an hour, wrap things up and close in prayer.
- Encourage the girls to get the participants guide for further study on their own.

If you'd like step-by-step guidance for starting an ETC Mentoring group, visit this link: http://www.moretobe.com/etc/.

Sunday School Class or Youth Group Breakout

If you'd like to use this resource at church or with a youth group, I'd recommend following the Bible Study schedule, but splitting the chapters over two weeks to make it a 10-week study in one of these two ways:

- Reading the chapter before the class: Instead of using all the questions in one session, you can pick a few questions to focus in the first session and the remainder in the following session.

- Reading the chapter during the class: Use the first session for reading the chapter together, and the second session for discussion of the questions.

Girls Retreat or a Mother-Daughter Retreat

This would be an amazing topic to cover in a girl's retreat or mother-daughter event. You could choose to do each chapter as individual sessions for a total of four sessions. You might also choose to skip the last chapter to reduce your time to three sessions. Then the third chapter can be sent home, to help the content really sink in and combat the week-after-a-retreat tailspin.

It is my desire that you take this material and make it your own. Come up with as many creative ways as possible to do this study, so that the girls in your world will be impacted by your gifts, too. And, be sure to share your ideas. I'd love to hear from you and share your creativity and input with our M2B Mentoring Network (You can learn more the *M2B Mentoring Network* and how to join here: http://www.moretobe.com/m2b-mentoring-network/). Speaking of which, if you'd like to receive some mentoring training to prepare you to lead this study, be sure to check out our amazing offerings at *More to Be* (http://www.moretobe.com/m2b-mentoring-training-study-options/).

Don't Go It Alone

As you get ready to launch forward in this study, I want you to know you're not alone. I'm here, rooting for you. My team of women at *More to Be* are commited to praying for you to confidently rise up and impact this next generation. You are backed up by us, but more importantly, you are appointed by God for this opportunity and strengthened by Christ working in you. The Holy Spirit is your ultimate guide, and will show you what to do and say step-by-step.

Even though you might feel pretty confident about stepping out to lead a group of girls through this study on your own, I want to also encourage you to find a partner. Years ago, I had a dear friend remind me that although I'm capable to do much on my own, God did not design me to be a renigade ministry warrior.

She urged me to find partners to co-labor with,
instead of taking off as I wished without the support
or blessings of being connected with the body of Christ.

Well, that was fabulous advice! Just look at the *More to Be* team and you'll see what I mean (http://www.moretobe.com/the-team/). I get to partner with these amazing women because one woman was bold enough to remind me that I needed the body of Christ to do this with — and so do you.

I encourage you to pray about what it means to partner with one other sister in Christ as you begin to lead this study in a group setting. (If you are doing this alone with your daughter, seek out one other woman to pray for you!) Ask God to show you at least one woman who could bring her gifts and talents to partner with yours.

Maybe she could host and you lead.

Maybe she could be available for one-on-one conversations with the girls.

Maybe she could be a prayer warrior.

Maybe she could handle the communications or make the sweets.

She doesn't have to be your friend or spiritual equal. Maybe she's someone that needs to get plugged into ministry again, after being out for a season. Or maybe she's a gal looking for some mentoring and training, and this is an opportunity for you to impact two generations at once.

I pray that as you look ahead and start planning, you'll remember that you're not in this alone and that it is quite possible God has in mind for you to bring someone else along on the journey.

May I send you forward with a blessing?

Heavenly Father, thank You so much for leading this special woman to this study. She is on the brink of launching forward on an exciting new journey and I ask for You to undergird her with confidence. You've pricked her heart to impact the next generation and I pray that You would be showing her exactly how, when, and where. Speak to her, Lord, with clarity and vision. Cause her spirit to be tender to Your leading and sensitive to the times when You might take her down unexpected paths. Guard her from the enemy's attacks. Put a shield of protection around her mind, body, and family. Give her Your victory over strongholds that may get in the way of this study. Fill her with Your zeal to see the Gospel shared with humility and grace. In Jesus' Name, Amen.

Before You Turn the Page

Take this moment to dedicate this study to the Lord
and lay your hopes before Him.

Use the prompts below to record your thoughts.

I give this study to you, Lord. . .

I hope that through this experience, I will learn. . .

I hope that through serving this way, I will see. . .

I am trusting You, Lord, to meet this need. . .

GET READY CHECKLIST

Two Weeks Ahead of Time

- Send out invitations, which can be in the form a traditional invitation, a flier, or a simple email, text, or phone call.
- Order books for participants or give them the instructions to order for themselves.
- Meet to pray with co-leader, co-host, or prayer partner.

One Week Ahead of Time

- Send an email reminder to the girls to get their books.
- Read all of the Introduction and pray about your focus for the first session.
- Pick activities to do.
- Shop for any supplies, including pens, index cards, and tissues.
- Don't forget to have tea, cups, sugar, milk and a carafe for the hot water.
- Consider picking up a sweet treat.
- Spend time in prayer and doing the study for yourself.
- Send a text or email reminder the day before.

Meeting Time

- Have on hand Bibles along with extra pens or pencils.
- Don't forget to boil the water for tea. . . yes, I've forgotten on occasion!
- Enjoy this journey and remember, you're doing it for the Lord!

INTRODUCTION

The Journey Awaits

Ephesians 2:10 NLT
For we are God's masterpiece.
He has created us anew in Christ Jesus,
so we can do the good things he
planned for us long ago.

The Game Plan
- Greet the Girls
- Tea Time!
- Gather together and do a get to know you game.
- Share your faith story and why you want to lead them through this study.
- Explain what to expect.
- Answer questions.
- Close in prayer.

Can you think of a time when you showed up at a place where no one knew you? Maybe it was the first day at a brand new school or drop-off time at sleepaway camp. Or maybe you enrolled in a special art class or signed up to serve at the local community center. No matter how you got to that place, the fact is no one knew who you were.

Would you introduce yourself as the dancer or reader?

A great artist or a brilliant science student?

As a Christ-follower or a faith skeptic?

In some ways, being "new" provides an opportunity for you to recreate yourself. If your old school friends might have called you the loner girl, maybe in your new school you try to become the social butterfly. Or if you got an unwanted reputation because of a bad "boy" decision, now could be your chance to begin again.

But more important than who you WERE is finding out who you ARE!

I'm not saying the past doesn't matter. Oh it does. Our decisions have the ability to impact our future. (Hang tight, because I'll share with you about how that happened to me later on.) Since we can't change the past, we have to face this day, and tomorrow, with an understanding of who we are. We need to figure out our identity because what we believe about ourselves will impact our decisions and how we go about living the life God has given us.

Our identity can either cause us to curl up in a corner, feeling worthless and rejected, or call us to step out in bold, courageous faith to do *that thing* we long to accomplish.

Don't misunderstand me, though. I'm not saying *that thing* should define us. We need to find our identity — how we define ourselves — in what God has to say about us. When we understand His truth, then we can make decisions that enable us to accomplish *that thing* with a godly purpose.

Who we are is really a matter of Whose we are.

Our identity is established by God as we enter into a relationship with His son, Jesus Christ. When we put our faith in Jesus, by believing that He died on the cross for our sin, we receive a brand new identity that comes from being a member of the family of God.

> *Ephesians 2:10 NLT*
> *For we are God's masterpiece. He has created us anew in Christ Jesus, so we can do the good things he planned for us long ago.*

As Ephesians 2:10 describes, ". . . we are God's masterpiece. . . created anew. . . ", but do you know what this means? Do you know what God made you for? Does asking this question frighten you? Or do you think it is pointless to even consider the purpose God has for your life?

According to the Bible, God says we are His precious daughters, masterpieces, made even more beautiful by faith in Christ. He receives us as we are and wants to make us more. . . more like Him. He wants to use our perfectly-designed lives for His purposes. And it is

10

in discovering that purpose that we begin to experience the journey to freedom we crave.

I've learned through my own life experiences, and in mentoring teen girls for more than 17 years, that having a sense about why God made us and how He may want to use us is extremely important. Knowing our purpose helps us make wise decisions and avoid the foolish ones, too. But before we can find our purpose, we have to first figure out who we are — we have to know what we believe about ourselves, God, and this world. And that, girls, begins with discovering our identity.

Together, we're going to look at what we believe about ourselves, what God says about who we are, how we're impacted by what others have to say about us, and how we can live in the freedom of embracing our identity in Christ. That's the journey to freedom, girls!

Heavenly Father, thank You that You made us as YOUR masterpiece. God help us to truly believe and accept the truth that You have made us brand new through faith in Your son, Jesus Christ. God, You have good plans for our lives — things that You planned long ago. Help us to remember this truth as we consider our identity today. In Jesus' Name, Amen.

Conversation Starters

Now would be a great time to get the girls talking about identity using these conversation starters:

• If you were going to introduce yourself at a party, what would you say?

• Do you feel confident or nervous about introducing yourself?

• Can you think of a time in which you pretended to be different than who you really are?

• What are some of the good things you think God made you to do?

• What excites you about this journey to freedom? What scares you?

CHAPTER ONE

Upside Down Freedom

2 Corinthians 5:17 NIV
Therefore, if anyone is in Christ,
the new creation has come:
The old has gone, the new is here!

I remember the very moment I found out I was accepted into *the one* college I was waiting to hear from. . . waiting for what seemed like forever. Literally, weeks after all the other acceptance letters arrived, I finally found *the one* in my mailbox. I ran up the driveway excited to share the good news, even though there was no one home to tell. I can't remember what I did next, but I'm sure I called a friend or my mom at work. What I do remember, however, was thinking. . .

> *"Finally, I'm free. I get to live the rest of my life exactly how I want to live it. I get a clean slate, a fresh start, a new beginning."*

Well, if only that was the truth. I wasn't as free as I thought I would be, and it was my own fault. In the weeks leading up to college, I made a really bad decision to start seriously dating a guy from my high school — a guy I had refused since the spring of my senior year. The same guy I turned down going to the prom with because he was rebounding out of a serious relationship. The same guy I wouldn't date because I had this policy to not get involved with anyone at my after-school job. But this guy pursued me hard, and I gave in.

GET READY CHECKLIST

One Week Ahead of Time
- Spend time in prayer and doing the study for yourself.
- Pick activities to do.
- Shop for any supplies.
- Consider picking up a treat.
- Make sure you have enough tea, cups, sugar, and milk.
- Send a text or email reminder the day before.

Meeting Time
- Have on hand Bibles along with extra pens or pencils.
- Don't forget to boil the water for tea.
- Focus your mind on pleasing the Lord and loving on the girls for His glory.

13

Girls, we like to be pursued, which inevitably makes us vulnerable and sometimes even foolish.

It's still amazing to me that I could go from "NO way" to "Bring it on!" — what on earth happened to me? Suddenly, I thought this was the man of my dreams, and I gave him all of mine. We planned our future marriage and discussed the names of our babies. I was romanced right into fairy-tale land and gave up everything for this boy . . . everything, if you know what I mean.

There I was as a college freshman, thinking I was so free to do whatever I wanted with my life, but in reality I was interlocking my soul with another human being who had no intentions of caring for me forever. Within six months, we broke up (my initiative), because I knew I lost the essence of myself in this relationship. I was crumbling into the shadows of this guy, watching my dreams dashed and stomped on by a boy not worthy of sharing them with me. It was either get out with whatever I had left, or stick with the biggest mistake of my life.

In the weeks to follow, I really learned how foolish I had been to date him in the first place. Can you believe he was cheating on me with his ex-girlfriend, who attended another college in the region? Talk about feeling crushed and humiliated. My worth felt the size of pea. Maybe even smaller. All these thoughts formed in my head and heart, like:

I'm not even worth being loved.
I can never trust anyone again.
I'm nothing but used goods.
I'll never be able to use those names for my children now.
Maybe I'll never even be a mom.
Will I ever find someone to love me and not betray me?

I'm not sure how I made it through the next few months without making any more life-changing, foolish decisions. Looking back, I'm sure

14

God's hand was on my life, even before I knew Him personally. Maybe it was the loss of love and sense of self-worth that God used to lure me into a search for something more. The break-up and betrayal was like a bucket of cold water thrown onto my life, leaving me skeptical and guarded in my all my relationships — even with friends. I'm sure, however, that's why I noticed something different in the lives of my summer camp co-workers. There was this group that seemed to have authenticity and a sense of purpose in their lives. They were the ones that skipped happy hour at the local bar on Friday nights, and instead invited me to join them at a church youth event. Even though they knew I didn't share the same philosophy about God, they were willing to spend time with me.

I look back and can see how they loved me with the fullness of Christ's love, and patiently waited for me to recognize Him in them. That's what made me want to know more about their faith and about this God they seemed to love so much. But I was still hesitant to give up my lifestyle and my "other" friends. I tried to balance both worlds but this thing inside of me knew it couldn't be that way forever.

In the fall of my junior year of college, I headed off for a semester in London, and I took with me questions about God and faith and the influences of those summer camp friends. I began to see life through a new lens. I watched my new London roomies make decisions that left them feeling frustrated, disappointed, and guilty. Sometimes, I made those foolish choices, too. Each time, my mind would circle back around to my camp friendships. Each time, I wanted more of what they had.

If my freedom led to foolish decisions and their lack of freedom led to a happier life, then was the freedom I wanted really freedom at all?

That was the question on my heart when I got the news about the death of one of my camp friend's moms. It sent me into a tailspin, even though we knew her battle with cancer was fierce. A week later, I received a Bible in the mail from the friend who shared the news with

FRIEND TIME

Friends have power and influence over our girls. Now is an opportunity to challenge the girls to consider what their friends are doing for them. Ask questions like these:

- How are your friends encouraging you to get to know God for yourself?

- How are your friends pulling you away from growing in your faith?

- What type of friend would others consider you to be?

- What needs to change in your life regarding friendships?

15

CHECK the PULSE

As you approach the important topic of salvation, be sensitive to the leading of the Holy Spirit. Be patient on the Lord and seek His direction, as you humbly walk alongside your girls:

- Look for an opportunity to share your salvation story.

- Encourage one of your girls to share their experience.

- Consider what it is like to feel like you don't have a salvation story, especially if you've been raised in a Christian home.

- Provide an opportunity for girls to make a commitment to Christ.

me. He wanted me to find comfort in the promises of heaven and the truths found in Scripture, but all it did was frustrate me. So I turned to a new friend, Susie, who lived upstairs. I could tell she was a Christian because she was just like my camp friends. . . and a pastor's kid, too.

I went up to her room and threw the Bible on the bed. I challenged her to tell me what it all meant, and she did the most unlikely thing. She said, "Forget the Bible for a minute." Instead, she asked me a question. . .

"How do you think you're getting into heaven?"

"Umm. Hmm. Well, I don't think I am!" I replied.

Susie asked me why, and I explained that I thought I broke too many of God's rules. And then she told me the sweetest truth I've ever heard.

***God wants your heart.
Not just your rule-following. He wants you to
believe that His son, Jesus, died on the cross
for the forgiveness of your sins — all those times you
broke those rules — so that you could spend
eternity with Him in heaven.***

Really? This was news to me and, to be honest, it sounded awesome. What a relief to be off the hook, simply by telling God that I believe in my heart that Jesus died for me and all my crazy sins.

Romans 10:9-10 NIV
If you declare with your mouth, "Jesus is Lord," and believe in your heart that God raised him from the dead, you will be saved. For it is with your heart that you believe and are justified, and it is with your mouth that you profess your faith and are saved.

As you might have figured out, I made the decision that night to believe in Jesus and to start living for Him. What I didn't know back then, however, is that God was going to radically change my life from the

16

inside out.

That freedom I craved — to live on my
own, to be my own boss, to find my own
happiness — was replaced with a
desire to live for Him.

Sure, it was a slow start. My habits didn't change at first. My life looked exactly the same the next morning as it did all the days leading up to that moment I said YES to Jesus. But within months, I recognized that if I was going to be an authentic follower of Jesus, I needed to figure out who He really was and what it mean to live for Him.

What I found out is that as I gave up my own freedom and embraced following Christ, I found the purpose and direction I always craved . . . the freedom to really live my life to the fullest. That's upside down freedom, friends! And it's the freedom we crave deep within our souls!

With each passing day, I made new choices about how I was going to live — from the words the came out of my mouth (like giving up cussing) to how I'd be in relationships with guys (choosing purity). As the Bible describes it, I was a new creation and learning how to live like such.

2 Corinthians 5:17 NIV
Therefore, if anyone is in Christ, the new creation has come: The old has
gone, the new is here!

Even though my life on the outside changed to reflect my new relationship with God, there was still this place in my heart and mind stuck on believing lies. I didn't yet know how to take my thoughts captive and certainly had no idea how to embrace my identity in Christ.

I KNEW I was NEW but didn't
KNOW who I was NOW.

ILLUSTRATION TIME

As a way to illustrate the process of becoming a new creation, take the time to learn about the life-cycle of a butterfly. You can watch some neat videos and look at pictures at the sites listed below. If your session time allows, share what you've learned with the girls and show them a video.

- http:/youtu.be/7AUeM8Mbalk

- http://www.hawaiiswim.org/ business/TheButterfly/TheButterfly.html

- http://youtu.be/-Eo3C2u-dFE

- http://youtu.be/u2cE86AA1q0

17

ACTIVITY TIME

One of the key points in this chapter is for the girls to consider what's influencing their identity, and therefore their life choices. The "What's Influencing Your Identity?" questions are designed to get them thinking concretely about the influences upon them, so make sure this exercise is not skipped.

Encourage the girls to share what they discovered. If your girls are shy or hesitant to do so in a group setting, use index cards and turn it into guessing a game, such as writing down:

- What is your number one influence?

- How much time do you spend reading your Bible versus reading for fun?

- How much time do you spend hanging with friends versus praying?

In some ways, I was like a little girl playing dress up. I carried the title of Christian and did Christian things, like going to church and attending a Bible study, not really knowing what to think about myself or how those thoughts impacted how I lived. Do you ever feel this way? Well, don't despair! You don't have to live in the shell of a Christian life. First, you need to know God's forgiveness and grace is being held out for you, as it was for me. See, I needed to receive God's forgiveness and not continue to punish myself over the things I regretted doing.

> *Acts 13:38 NIV*
> *Therefore, my friends, I want you to know that through Jesus the forgiveness of sins is proclaimed to you.*

I also had to learn how to live in light of God's grace, receiving this gift even though I felt I didn't deserve it. Receiving it for the past and the present.

> *Ephesians 2:8-9 NIV*
> *For it is by grace you have been saved, through faith—and this is not from yourselves, it is the gift of God— not by works, so that no one can boast.*

Once I embraced God's forgiveness and grace, I still needed to learn how to live differently. And so do you! It's a process that requires changing our thinking so that our habits will change, too. And that change begins with an influences inventory. What do I mean by that? Well, read on.

What's Influencing Your Identity?

I think it is safe to say that one of the reasons we really struggle with knowing our identity in Christ is because we are all too easily influenced by *what* others say about us and by *what* we think of our own accomplishments or actions. We're also influenced by *what* takes up our time, so we need to think seriously about *how* we spend our time, too.

Take a few minutes to think about how your worth has been defined by checking off each statement that is true for you:

_____ what my friends say about me

_____ what my parents think about me

_____ what my teachers say about me

_____ what my boyfriend thinks of me

_____ what my coaches or instructors think of me

_____ what my pastor thinks of me

_____ what my youth leader thinks of me

_____ what I think about myself

_____ what God thinks of me

As you look at this list, can you recognize who has the most influence on you?

Can you see how you're motivated to believe certain things about yourself based on your relationships?

If you had to put this list in priority order, which opinion gets the number one position? The last position?

Is that really the way it should be?

Beside the people in your life, you are also influenced by how you spend your time, so let's figure out where all your time is going to. Jot down the minutes/hours invested in the blank:

watching TV _____

listening to non-Christian music_____

listening to Christian music_____

reading for fun_____

surfing the internet_____

shopping_____

19

hanging with friends_____

school work_____

working out_____

reading your Bible_____

praying_____

church_____

serving others by choice_____

leadership responsibilities_____

time with family_____

What do you spend most of your time doing?

What do you spend the least amount of your time doing?

Can you see how those "time consumers" are impacting your identity and sense of worth?

What do you think should change so that you can more clearly embrace your identity in Christ?

It's Time to Run Free

If we really want to experience the freedom to live our lives as God has designed us to, we need to start with realizing how we are affected by others and our experiences. We have to investigate what we think and why we think that way in the first place.

> *We have to know our beliefs and really*
> *figure out if they are true. Why?*
> *Because what we think influences how we live.*

Our beliefs about ourselves, this world, and God impact how we define ourselves — and that definition determines our identity. If our identity is based on our accomplishments or relationships, then it is forever changing. But if our identity is based on the unchangeable Truth, then we can move through the highs and lows of life without being crushed or thrown off course.

Think about how one ordinary day could go entirely wrong, like:

Something ugly happened with a friend at school . . .
Your parents are mad about your low grade in history . . .
The boy you like asked someone else to the semi-formal . . .
There's a giant pimple forming right next to your nose . . .

In that moment, when all those issues are happening to YOU, you feel anything but valuable and worthy. Instead you feel like poop. Yes, I just said a potty word. But isn't that the truth? So what should you do — in that very, poopy feeling moment?

It's in that moment that your identity matters most, especially when it is shaped and established by what God says about you. That's when you have to kick to the curb any lie spinning through your mind and embrace your identity in Christ, as it is defined throughout the Bible. Truths like:

> *You are made in the image of God!*
> *Christ died on the cross for your*
> *sin . . . their sin . . . that sin!*
> *You are a child of God and He loves you!*
> *You are not defined by how you feel,*
> *or where you failed,*
> *but by your holy status*
> *that God has given you!*
> *Your inheritance in Christ equips*
> *you with power to overcome this mess!*

STOP & SHARE

Take time to think about how you've felt when things don't go according to plan or when life tosses you a curve ball. Consider some examples from your life that you could share with the girls:

- How do your feelings impact your decisions and habits?

- Do you have some unhealthy habits worth changing?

- What helps you make wise choices even when you feel awful?

21

AS GOES THE MENTOR

Are you ready to get uncomfort-able, friends? As we start talking with our girls about the impor-tance of reading the Bible daily, we have to be ready to live out what we teach. So, let me present a couple of ways for you to do this with integrity:

Option 1.

If you struggle with daily Bible reading, confess to the girls about what this is like for you personally. Take the challenge with them to commit to a Bible reading plan.

Option 2.

If you've found success and joy in reading your Bible daily, share with the girls how you started that habit. Also show them what you do and communicate what you get out of it, too.

Your position in the family of God means you don't need to go through it alone, but can depend on others around you!

Because of what God has given us through Jesus, we can live with hope, purpose, and the promise of overcoming! But understanding this truth requires a study of Scripture to find out exactly what God says. We will also need the encouragement of Christian mentors, parents, and friends who can help us learn how to read the Word and learn it for ourselves!

You Need a Plan

If you're like the teenage girls I get to mentor, then I'm betting reading your Bible is not exactly something you love doing. Maybe you don't even know where to start, so that's why our first step in the journey to freedom is for you to learn how to read it on your own. It's one thing for me to tell you what the Bible says is true, but what if you want to know something I haven't covered? What if you want to learn something I've not taught you? You need to know the Scriptures for your-self! You need to know how to use God's Word as your journey map.

While there are so many different techniques and study methods, I want to give you one that is super simple and easily accomplished. So are you ready for the challenge?

1. *Pick a Bible or Bible App*

There are so many Bibles and Bible Apps to choose from, so let me suggest these three options, which I believe are the best:

- NIV Compact Student Bible {available on Amazon}
- NIV Life Application Study Bible {available on Amazon}
- Olive Tree App - http://www.olivetree.com/

22

Our ministry also provides an online resource guide to help you find just the right bible for your studies: http://www.moretobe. com/2011/08/23/finding-a-bible/

2. *Get a Journal or Notebook*

Get creative and personalize a notebook or binder, or pick up an inexpensive journal.

3. *Pick a Book of the Bible*

Ideally, you can make it a goal to read the whole Bible, one chapter at a time. Yes, this will take you a few years, but what's the rush? Don't know where to start? How about beginning with the list below to get started. The books suggested rotate between the short letters written by Paul, the Gospels, Psalms, Proverbs, and a few Old Testament gems.

- Ephesians
- John
- Psalms
- Philippians
- Genesis
- Matthew
- Galatians
- Proverbs
- Luke
- Jeremiah
- Colossians
- Mark
- 1 Timothy & 2 Timothy

• Isaiah

4. *Read a Chapter a Day*

You can choose to read as much or as little as you'd like, but I find a chapter a day is totally doable. You'll feel like you completed something and can easily mark in your Bible where you left off.

5. *Write Down What Stands Out*

You may think reading is just enough, but there is something that happens in the brain when we actually write down what we're learning. You don't have to take pages and pages of notes. Just write down something like this:

- Date
- Chapter
- Theme of the Chapter
- Main Characters
- What did the main characters do right or wrong?
- What did they learn from what happened?
- What can we learn from what happened?
- What verse(s) really stands out personally?

At first, your commitment to read your Bible may not seem to be accomplishing much, but imagine if you decided to stop washing your hair. For a day or two, it might not be noticeable. But over a week, well, you'd start to notice. Over a month, and well, that would be pretty bad, right? In the same way, you may not notice the results of your Bible reading. It may not make sense to you. You might be totally confused and think the Scriptures are completely irrelevant. But trust me. In time, you'll see your knowledge increase and your understanding grow. You'll be changed by the truths of Scriptures. It may take days, months, years, but it will happen.

Let me just make this clear.
It will take years to see God's transforming
work in your life, but it is worth the
investment of your time!

I've been reading my Bible almost every day for the last 10 years (yes, that means I didn't do that for the first 10 years of being a Christian) and I still have a ton to learn. I still don't know things, which motivates me to keep on reading and learning from others. That's the journey of faith, girls. You could take an entire lifetime of reading the Scriptures, and there will still be more to discover about God. But imagine if you start now! Imagine what God will do in your life and through your life. Imagine!

Girls, the Lord has called you to be His child and equips you to live this life with His great purposes in mind. It is such a worthy calling in which you get to experience God's power, strength, hope, and joy, no matter your circumstances.

God doesn't promise a happy life,
but He promises us a full one!

You'll forever be an imperfect mess, and that is okay. Your life will have problems, but they don't need to define you. Instead, God can work through them — and through you — to show the world His hope and purposes. No matter what you've done in the past, or what mistakes you'll make in the future, your identity in Christ can never be marred. So would you be willing to embrace what God says about you? Will you choose to believe His truth over your feelings? Will you live in the freedom of being you. . . as God defines you?

Heavenly Father, thank You for this journey of freedom that You've
given us the privilege to experience. It is so different than what
we expect. It is something we have to receive with a measure of

ACCOUNTABILITY

Take the time to find out where your girls are in their Bible reading habit and what sort of commitment they would like to make going forward. Present some fun options for accountability, like:

Party Reward. . .

Have an ice cream party after everyone finishes reading their Bible for two weeks in a row.

Project Reward. . .

Make something as a reward for completing a 30-day challenge of Bible reading, such as crafting a bracelet or tie-dying a t-shirt.

Keep each other accountable by texting or emailing a Bible verse from each day's reading.

25

faith and hope, as we give up what we think we know is true and embrace what You say is true. God, help us through this study, to discover what your Word says about us. Help us to find our identity in Christ and live our lives with the promises of Your purposes established in our hearts. In Jesus' Name, Amen.

A PLAN TO STRETCH

There are a two different ways you can help your girls make the most of the "Time to Stretch" questions. Pick the option that best suits you as the leader, the dynamics of the girls participating in the study, and the way you are using the study (Bible Study versus Mentoring Group format).

Option 1 - Bible Study Format

If the girls completed the chapter reading and questions for before your study time, use the questions as conversation prompts. Encourage the girls to share their answers with the group. If they are quiet and hesitant, use index cards for them to jot down their answers anonymously and then read aloud.

Option 2 - Mentoring Gathering Format

If the girls have arrived without having read the chapter or answering the questions, you can choose to use the questions as a homework option for the girls. You can find printable downloads of the chapter questions for each week at http://www.moretobe.com/freedom-resources.

Option 3 - Time Sensitive Needs

If your meeting time is less than an hour, you may choose to do the chapter content and questions over two different sessions.

Time to Stretch Questions

1. Would you say you crave freedom, and if so, how would you describe what you're longing for?

2. Do you think God promises you freedom? Or have you always thought of God as taking away your freedom? How has your opinion been challenged through what you've read so far?

3. Our identity is not found in what we do each day nor by what others say about us, who we are in a relationship with or who we hang

out with. Our identity is found in our place in the family of God, made possible by faith in Jesus Christ as our personal Savior. Have you received Jesus as your Savior? If yes, please take this moment to record your experience and thank God for this gift. If no, take time to tell God what makes you hold back or hesitate, and ask Him to increase your faith.

EXPLAINING SALVATION

As you listen to the hearts of your girls describing their faith journey, you may feel insecure about explaining the Gospel in a clear and concise way. These resources will help you and can be made available to your girls, as well:

• Ready for a Change - http://www.moretobe.com/meet-jesus/

• PeacewithGod.net - http://peacewithgod.jesus.net/

You can also study these Scriptures so that you can share the journey of salvation personally:

• Ephesians 2:8-10
• Matthew 10:32-33
• I John 1:9
• Acts 2:38, 3:1
• Romans 5:1, 4:16, 1:16-17, 10:9-13, 8:5-11, 2:4-5, 6:1-8, 12:1-2

4. If we want to know our identity in Christ, we can find it clearly laid out in Ephesians 1. Read the whole chapter below and then check

off all the statements that describe your identity.

_____ blessed

_____ chosen

_____ holy

_____ blameless

_____ predestined

_____ adopted

_____ redeemed

_____ forgiven

_____ rich in grace

_____ included in Christ

_____ saved

_____ marked

_____ knowing the truth

_____ able to believe

_____ sealed

_____ God's possession

_____ guaranteed our inheritance

_____ the praise of His glory

_____ filled with the Holy Spirit

5. How do the descriptions from the Ephesians 1 passage change your definition of what it means to be a child of God? (Did you check

everyone? They're all correct!) How does it impact your identity in a good way?

6. Are you willing to make the commitment to read a chapter a day in the Bible and record what you discover? If yes, please share this decision with a Christian friend, mentor, or parent. Ask them to hold you accountable to the goals you write down below:

   1. I plan to use this Bible or App:

   2. I plan to have my journal and notebook ready to use by this date:

   3. I plan to read this book in the Bible:

   4. I plan to read a chapter a day, which means I'd like to finish

reading the book I selected by this date:

5. I plan to write down what I am reading and would like to show my notes to my accountability partner by this date:

Visit http://www.moretobe.com/freedom-resources for chapter-by-chapter resources and links.

PARTNERSHIP

Take time to challenge the girls to set some goals for their Bible reading along with developing accountability partnerships. Brainstorm options, such as:

- pairing up in the group
- asking a sister, aunt, grandma
- connecting with a friend who moved away

Also, encourage the girls to be specific about how they'll be accountable to their partners, such as:

- using email and texting
- meeting once a week
- scheduling a phone call

Challenge the girls to set a date and plan a reward:

- pick a goal date
- pick a reward
- set a consequence, too

CHAPTER TWO

Take Your Mark

1 Corinthians 9:24 NIV
Don't you realize that in a race everyone runs,
but only one person gets the prize?
So run to win!

When the gun fires at the start of a track meet, everyone knows what just happened. The racers take off out of the starting blocks with their eyes locked in on the finish line. Whether running a 50-yard dash or 4 x 4 relay, they know why they are there and what they're supposed to be doing. Run! Run for the prize!

> *1 Corinthians 9:24 NIV*
> *Don't you realize that in a race everyone runs, but only one person gets the prize? So run to win!*

But imagine if the runners showed up unprepared? Think of the shock if a county champion showed up in flip-flops and a bikini? Would she be prepared for her race without her track sneakers or uniform on? Or imagine a state qualifying sprinter talking on the phone instead of getting her feet in the blocks as the gun is about to go off! We'd think she was crazy, right? She'd lose the race for sure!

Well now, stretch your imagination beyond the track meet, because there's another really important race you should think about. See, your life is like a long distance race, for which you train every single day.

33

GET READY CHECKLIST

One Week Ahead of Time
- Spend time in prayer and doing the study for yourself.
- Pick activities to do.
- Shop for any supplies.
- Consider picking up a treat.
- Make sure you have enough tea, cups, sugar, and milk.
- Send a text or email reminder the day before.

Meeting Time
- Have on hand Bibles along with extra pens or pencils.
- Don't forget to boil the water for tea.
- Keep looking to the Lord for direction and His wisdom.

You have to learn how to build up your endurance and condition your body. You have to learn how to get in the mental game and know your own strengths and weakness. You'll have to figure out what to do to prepare for success and what to do when you face failure, too. That's why the Bible compares our life of faith to that of an athlete running a race.

> *Hebrews 12:1-2 NLT*
> *Therefore, since we are surrounded by such a huge crowd of witnesses to the life of faith, let us strip off every weight that slows us down, especially the sin that so easily trips us up. And let us run with endurance the race God has set before us. We do this by keeping our eyes on Jesus, the champion who initiates and perfects our faith.*

God wants us to embrace this life He's given us with as much dedication and purpose as that champion athlete showing up for the state qualifying meet. We need to know how to "take our mark" so that we can run this race well. And that starts with knowing how we've been marked — in a good way — by God for this world. It starts with knowing our identity.

Wait a Minute

Before we go any further, let me tell you why I know so much about this "running the race" thing. See, back when I was in high school, I spent a season on the track team. Well, that was only because I'd been injured so many times that I couldn't do what I was really passionate about — dance. After 13 years of dance, I had to give up my dream of one day being a Rockette {I know, a big silly dream}, because I tore up my knees one too many times.

After so many years of being physically active, I couldn't quit sports all-together, but the options were limited. The doctor recommended swimming and running. In the fall, I joined the swim team and did pretty well for a rookie, and in the spring I found myself on the track team, even though I couldn't run to save my life. Slow doesn't even begin to describe my trot back then, and my long distance ability was equally disappointing. So, my very patient track coach sent me in a new direction. He suggested I become a race walker, and to everyone's surprise, I actually did quite well. I figured out the technique, practiced somewhat diligently, and was ready to be my high school's next star athlete.

At the start of my very first race, the gun went off and I sprinted ahead, edging past the other competitors. Shockingly, I continued to gain on them and captured first place as though I'd been race walking for years. It could have been an amazing celebration. *Could have.* If only I hadn't been disqualified. Yes, I was disqualified because I had spandex leggings on under my running shorts and that was against the rules.

Apparently, I wasn't as prepared to compete as I should have been. It wasn't just about conditioning and mindset. I needed to know the rules, too.

The details matter — which is a truth that pertains to every area of life.

You could say that my little experience with race walking became quite an important life lesson. I learned, in a slightly painful but not life-altering way, that I need to pay attention to the details in every area of my life — especially when it comes to my faith and what God says to us through the Bible. And the Bible was something I didn't know about at all when I was your age. I didn't grow up in a Christian home, and was a crazy teenager who made more than a few bad decisions. When I accepted Jesus as my Savior in college, I had a lot to learn about who God is and what it means to be His child. I've had to really pay attention to what the Bible said about my identity in Christ, because so much of what I believed about myself was formed through what others said — the good, the bad, and the ugly. All those words impacted my life, and not always in a good way.

In the same way I should have paid attention to the race walking rules so that I could have won the race, I've also come to see that God's Word will give me everything I need to be able to run this faith-life race in such a way as to experience the blessing of win.

35

STOP & SHARE

Have you recently faced a disappointment because you were unprepared or missed the details?

Can you remember a time when you were a teen in which you thought you knew what you were doing, but really didn't and got yourself in trouble?

Take time to consider a relevant story of your own to share with your girls. Feel free to leave out the details and focus on the lessons learned in the process.

Hebrews 4:12 NIV
For the word of God is alive and active. Sharper than any double-edged
sword, it penetrates even to dividing soul and spirit, joints and marrow; it
judges the thoughts and attitudes of the heart.

I want you to be able to run strong and able, confident and prepared, passionate about finishing well. I want you to know what God says is true, so that you'll have no regrets about how you run this life-race God has given you.

So who are you?

Knowing your identity is like knowing the rules of the race. Identity is about discovering who you are according to what God says is true, and then living in that truth without compromise. This is the key to being authentic and confident, the real deal and not a phony, true to yourself and not swayed by the crowd.

According to Dictionary.com, identity is:

> "The condition of being oneself or itself, and not another; condition or character as to who a person or what a thing is; the sense of self, providing sameness and continuity in personality over time; the state of having unique identifying characteristics held by no other person or thing; the individual characteristics by which a person or thing is recognized."

Most people assume that identity is about fancy titles, degrees, and accomplishments, like class president, captain of the soccer team, graduate with honors, PhD, senator, or published author. But these titles don't point to a person's identity. Rather, they describe a person's accomplishments or responsibilities.

> ***Identity is about your God-given uniqueness***
> ***manifested in the plans He has for your life.***

36

You are not an accident or a mistake. Everything from how you look, your personality, passions, strengths, weaknesses, gifts and talents are all a part of God's master design. There is no one else like you! He set you apart as one of His fearfully and wonderfully made creations, designed to be used for a good purpose, right here, right now.

> *Psalm 139:14 MSG*
> *Oh yes, you shaped me first inside, then out;*
> *you formed me in my mother's womb.*
> *I thank you, High God—you're breathtaking!*
> *Body and soul, I am marvelously made!*
> *I worship in adoration—what a creation!*
> *You know me inside and out,*
> *you know every bone in my body;*
> *You know exactly how I was made, bit by bit,*
> *how I was sculpted from nothing into something.*
> *Like an open book, you watched me grow from conception to birth;*
> *all the stages of my life were spread out before you,*
> *The days of my life all prepared*
> *before I'd even lived one day.*

In order to really uncover your true identity, however, you need to figure out for yourself where your source of truth is going to come from.

Will it be God's Word or what others say?

Will it be through receiving Jesus as your Lord and Savior?

Will you receive God's gift of salvation — the promise that He's rescued you from your sin, saving you for heaven and giving you purpose for this life on earth?

Will you turn in another direction?

PAUSE TO ASK
Whether you're reading the chapter together or have been going through it independently, you can certainly use these questions for discussion time.

Maybe your decision should be based on what God says of you and what He promises to those who call Him Lord. Promises like these:

> *Ephesians 1:3-6 MSG*
> *How blessed is God! And what a blessing he is! He's the Father of our*

37

Master, Jesus Christ, and takes us to the high places of blessing in him.
Long before he laid down earth's foundations, he had us in mind, had
settled on us as the focus of his love, to be made whole and holy by his love.
Long, long ago he decided to adopt us into his family through Jesus Christ.
(What pleasure he took in planning this!) He wanted us to enter into the
celebration of his lavish gift-giving by the hand of his beloved Son.

If you accept your place in God's family, you no longer need to define
yourself by your own goodness. Instead, you can rest in God's grace.

Isn't it freeing to know that a perfect,
holy God can have room in His heart
for imperfect, but holy, children?

Yes, holy. I know that may surprise you, but holiness is the foundation
of your identity as a child of God.

Why Identity and Holiness Go Together

What do you think holiness means? Is it something that shouldn't be
touched? Or is it something religious? The word holy means "set apart
or sacred." That certainly describes God, right? We know He is holy,
because that is how the Bible describes Him.

> *Isaiah 6:3*
> *And they were calling to one another: "Holy, holy, holy is the LORD*
> *Almighty; the whole earth is full of his glory."*

Did you know holy is the only word repeated three times in a row to
describe God? I guess that means it is a pretty big deal. But what
does God's holiness have to do with you and your identity? Well let
me explain. It starts with Jesus, who also happens to also be holy. As
we read in Luke, when Jesus' birth was announced, He was called the
Holy One.

> *Luke 1:35*

The angel answered, "The Holy Spirit will come upon you, and the power of the Most High will overshadow you. So the holy one to be born will be called the Son of God."

Both God and Jesus are holy. When we become a part of God's family through faith in Christ, we become holy — this is part of our inheritance simply because God promises to work it out this way.

Hebrews 10:10, 14
And by that will, we have been made holy through the sacrifice of the body of Jesus Christ once for all. . . because by one sacrifice he has made perfect forever those who are being made holy.

As children within the family of God, we take on the attributes of our Father in heaven. It's kind of like the way a mother and daughter may sound alike, look alike, and even have the same mannerism. The mom doesn't have to try to make the daughter like her. It just happens! Maybe that's because through salvation, God also gives us the gift of the Holy Spirit to dwell within us.

Ephesians 1:13
And you also were included in Christ when you heard the word of truth, the gospel of your salvation. Having believed, you were marked in him with a seal, the promised Holy Spirit. . .

So, yes, we are holy through becoming part of God's family, and also marked by holiness through the Holy Spirit living within us. We are more than skin and bones brought into this world. We are more than the sum of all our accomplishments. We are more than the sordidness of all our sin. We are holy children of a holy God and we are called to live in a way that is holy.

1 Peter 1:15-16
But just as he who called you is holy, so be holy in all you do; for it is written: 'Be holy, because I am holy.'

You may be wondering, but how do I actually live holy? Does that mean I have to be perfect? No, not at all. But as a child of God, it is certainly reasonable to strive toward obeying God and pursuing a life of holiness — a life that is set apart. And, that girlfriend, is why knowing your identity in Christ is so important. It will influence your choices and the ways you choose to be set apart, different, and unique for all the right reasons. Yes, your holy status, your identity in Christ, will impact your friendships and who you date. It will affect where you want to work and who you might want to live with in college. It will even influence your career choice and the ways you choose to spend your free time. . . and financial resources. Did you know that being holy could ever mean so much?

Now Imagine a New Identity

Let's go back to imagining that moment when you've just showed up as the newbie. Pretend like you're going to a party this weekend, hosted by a good friend, but the guest list includes people you've never met before. You spend time figuring out what to wear and when to arrive, hoping to make a good first impression. When you walk in the front door, the crowd is loud and every corner of the house is packed with warm bodies. There's no hope of finding your friend, nor being able to stick with her for the evening. You'll have to get into the mix and introduce yourself again and again.

What will you say?

How will you describe yourself?

Will it be based on feelings?

Accomplishments?

Dreams?

Will you be honest?

Authentic?

Fake?

Transparent?

Chances are, you'll tell people your name and what you do, like

40

playing a sport or leading a club at school. You'll panic, trying to come up with an impressive list of things that describe you in order to feel more valuable. In the back of your mind, you might even think about what other people have said about you. That little voice in your head whispers. . .

> *I am so _____!*
>
> *If only I wasn't so _____!*
>
> *I wish I was _____!*

What would you fill your blank in with? Stupid, fat, ugly, smart, pretty, better, foolish, rebellious, perfect, insignificant, insecure, bad, good, worthless, hopeless, independent, needy, lonely, alone.
That may be how you feel, but are any of those thoughts consistent with your identity in Christ and your holy value?

Identity, my friend, is about who God says you are.

If God was given the chance to introduce you at the party, He would say things like:

> *She is MY Child. John 1:12, Romans 8:14-15*
>
> *She is Christ's friend. John 15:15*
>
> *She is MY workmanship. Ephesians 2:10*
>
> *She is MY coworker. 2 Corinthians 6:1*
>
> *She is chosen and appointed by MY son, Jesus Christ, to bear His fruit. John 15:16*
>
> *She is forgiven. Matthew 26:28, Ephesians 1:7*
>
> *She is sealed with the promised Holy Spirit. Ephesians 1:13*
>
> *She is a new creation. 2 Corinthians 5:17*

41

She is alive with Christ. Ephesians 2:5

She is blessed with every spiritual blessing in heavenly places. Ephesians 1:3

She is set free. Romans 8:2, John 8:32

She is not alone and does not need to fear. Isaiah 43:1-3, Deuteronomy 31:6-8

She is victorious through the Lord Jesus Christ. 1 Corinthians 15:57

She is not controlled by the sinful nature but by the Spirit. Romans 8:9

She knows my voice and follows me. John 10:27

She has received eternal life and cannot be snatched out of MY hand. John 10:28

She is able to hear MY voice. John 8:47

She does not belong to this world. John 15:19

She belongs to ME! 1 Peter 2:9

This is your true identity! What God says about you is who you really are, even when you don't feel like it. So how come these truths don't come to your mind first? Unfortunately, your identity is often shaped by the people and circumstances that have had the greatest influence upon you.

> ***Living with Truth as the foundation of your identity will entirely change your perspective about your life and purpose.***

Since we are so quick to listen, watch, and learn from the opinions and examples of others, it is all too easy to allow stinkin' thinkin' to affect our beliefs about ourselves and God. These lies counter God's truth, but until we recognize them as lies, they have power to negatively impact our identity and our life choices. That's why I'm going to spend the next chapter sharing with you about how to overcome stinkin' thinkin', so that you can embrace your true identity in Christ.

Heavenly Father, if those statements are really true about our identity, then why don't we feel that way? Will You show us how stinkin' thinkin' gets in the way? We ask You to open the eyes of our hearts so that we can soak in Your truth. We don't want to just learn information, but we want to have a new understanding and see our lives changed because of Your Truth. In Jesus' Name, Amen.

Time to Stretch Questions

1. What words would you use to describe your identity? Make one column of words that you would have chosen before reading this chapter and one column of new words that come to mind as a result of reading this chapter.

A PLAN TO STRETCH

Which option will work for you this week?

Option 1 -

Bible Study Format

- discuss the questions
- use index cards to help with sharing

Option 2 -

Mentoring Gathering Format

- download the questions from moretobe.com/freedom-resources
- send home with the girls

Option 3 -

Time Sensitive Needs

- send home the questions
- discuss in the next session

ACTIVITY TIME

This chapter and these questions provide a great opportunity to help the girls reshape their identity by God's Word.

You can use the "ID Cards" resources available at *More to Be* (http://www.moretobe.com/id-cards/) to do a craft project, such as:

- making banners for them to hang in their room
- decorating picture frames to place the ID Card inside
- creating ID note cards to share with family and friends

You can also supply craft paper and markers and have the girls make their own pictures using the "She is. . ." statements.

2. What does God say about you, according to Psalm 139? Write down the key phrases, words, and thoughts that you think define your identity.

3. Go back to your answers for question one. Can you see which words describe what others have said about you or to you about yourself? Which of those words are not consistent with what you wrote down as your answers to question two? Take a few minutes to journal about what this means to you, especially as you think about your identity.

4. In light of what you've learned through this chapter, describe why it would be a good idea to embrace a new, holy identity in Christ? How would this change the way you spend your time and who you hang out with?

5. Look up these verses in your Bible or on Biblegateway.com and jot down the full verse or something to help you remember what those verses are about. Pick out three that stand out to you. Write them down on post-it notes or index cards and tape them to your bedroom or bathroom mirror. Personalize the verses by using your name or "I" in the appropriate places:

- Psalm 139:1-4, 3-16

- John 1:12-13; 15:15

- 2 Corinthians 1:21-22; 5:17-21

- Ephesians 1:4-5; 2:10

- Philippians 3:20

- Colossians 2:13-14; 3:12

- 1 Peter 2:5, 9

Visit http://www.moretobe.com/freedom-resources for chapter-by-chapter resources and links.

CHAPTER THREE

Choosing to Believe

Romans 12:2 NIV
Do not conform any longer to the pattern of this world,
but be transformed by the renewing of your mind.

If you asked me what I honestly thought about myself when I was 16, I probably would have said something like this. . .

> *Well, I don't think I'm totally ugly or too fat or too dumb, but I'm not thin enough, pretty enough, smart enough to be good enough for* _____.

That blank could have been filled in with the name of the boy(s) I liked, my cheerleading coach, or even my parents. My perceptions were definitely shaped by what I thought others thought about of me. Looking back, I'm not surprised. As the new kid at school in fifth grade, I was teased about how I looked and even how hard I worked. In junior high, my grades kept me just out of reach of the honors classes. And, well, at home, things weren't so great. With my parents struggling in their marriage, it was easy to believe that their unhappiness had something to do with me.

What others said or did to me shaped my identity and stuck with me as a young adult. Even after becoming a Christian in college, I still had a warped perspective about myself and what I should be able to

GET READY CHECKLIST

One Week Ahead of Time
- Spend time in prayer and doing the study for yourself.
- Pick activities to do.
- Shop for any supplies.
- Consider picking up a treat.
- Make sure you have enough tea, cups, sugar, and milk.
- Send a text or email reminder the day before.

Meeting Time
- Have on hand Bibles along with extra pens and pencils.
- Don't forget to boil the water for tea.
- Remember to keep focused on doing this for the Lord!

STOP & SHARE

STOP & SHARE

Do you remember how you struggled with your identity as a teen? Do you still struggle with those beliefs and insecurities?

- Do you struggle with feeling like you're not enough?
- Do you feel pressure to please others?
- Are you insecure with your appearance?
- Do you doubt your abilities or qualifications?

Answer these questions honestly and prayerfully. Ask the Lord to speak to your heart and reveal areas that you need to give over to Him. You might even seek out the help of a Christian counsel or mentor.

Let your motivation be out of desire to be in a healthy place so that you can impact the next generation with Truth!

accomplish. I lived with a sense of regret and failure, listening to the opinions of others more than embracing the truth God offers us in the Bible. I'd say things like:

> *If only I could have fixed my parents' marriage, not made that stupid decision in my freshman year, gotten that score on the SATs, then I'd know I was good enough for _____ and wouldn't feel so stupid about _____ .*

While my focus shifted off my appearance, I was still fixated on my performance and abilities. My identity was so impacted by my sense of failure, that it actually kept me from trying new things and pursuing opportunities.

> ### *I put my life in a box and defined myself in a way that kept me from becoming who God wanted me to be.*

I suffered from stinkin' thinkin', which is when we allow anything but the Truth, as found in the Bible, to define ourselves. Our stinkin' thinkin' can form in all sorts of ways, from the seemingly insignificant moment when we were overlooked by our friends, to something way more traumatic, like the loss of parent. When life has dealt us these difficult experiences, imprint beliefs can be left on our hearts and minds, shaping how we see ourselves, God, and the world around us.

Stinkin' thinkin' can also be passed down from generation to generation, where there are certain beliefs or expectations within a family that form a mindset which is inconsistent with Scripture. Beliefs like these:

> *If you go to church every Sunday, God will be happy with you.*
>
> *If you recycle, that makes you a better Christian because you're taking care of the planet.*
>
> *If you get good grades, you will make the family look good.*
>
> *If you are a starter on the soccer team, those years of playing little league were worth the investment.*

If you keep your room messy, you're nothing but a slob in a pig sty.
If you have acne on your face, it's because you don't know how to take care of yourself.
If you go to youth group, you've got to be a Christian.

While some of these beliefs may have elements of truth in them, they are really false statements coming out of trying to prove worth and significance. The culture and media also offer their part in the warping of our thinking.

That cover girl model is so beautiful, but what did she look like before a graphic artist completely transformed what she looks like in real life?
That house on HGTV is so perfectly organized and decorated, but is that only because no one actually lives in it?
That character on a hit TV series seems to always have the perfect best friend, so why is she so lonely in her real life?
That couple on the cover of People magazine must be in love with the way they are looking at each other, so why are they really on the brink of divorce?
That Ivy League school promises a 6-figure job upon graduation, but at what cost?

These beliefs are not consistent with God's truth (John 17:17) and are lies that come straight from the devil, who is also called the Father of Lies (John 8:44).

John 17:17 NIV
Sanctify them by the truth; your word is truth.

So do you see how easy it is to be confused about our identity? Of course we're caught in between two worlds — truth and lies — because there is a spiritual battle waging for our lives. God wants us to experience the full life He has promised us, while the enemy, also called the thief, is out to steal, kill, and destroy us.

IS THIS YOU?
As you read through this chapter, you might begin to see that some of your beliefs are not rooted in the Truth. Please don't fall into despair or condemnation! I pray this chapter is the next step in helping you discern Truth!

I didn't know how to discern lies from the truth until I went through Life Breakthrough Academy's Life Coach Training program. The curriculum was foundational in teaching me to make sure what I believe lines up with the truth.

If you'd like to experience the training I did, even if you don't want to become a life coach, please do contact me and consider signing up for the next Life Coach Training course. It will help you grow as a follower of Christ!

John 10:10 NIV
The thief comes only to steal and kill and destroy; I have come that they
may have life, and have it to the full.

Satan is busy doing what he's done since the beginning of time. In the same way he tempted Eve in the Garden of Eden by causing her to doubt what God said, he continues to torment us with doubting God's truth and trying to make us believe that it is relevant to us today. Oh, but my friend, God's truth is timeless. His Word is full of wisdom and direction, hope and perspective.

I know this one teenage girl who has grown up in a Christian home, attended Sunday school since she was in diapers, and willingly goes to youth group. Yet, she struggles in her faith and swears the Bible is just too difficult to read. One the one hand, I agree with her. If you just pick up the Bible and try to make sense of it by focusing on only the verses that appeal to you, it can be pretty frustrating. It's like sitting down to watch a movie and fast-forwarding to a scene right in the middle. You have no idea what happened up to that point and forever wonder what was going on. Actually, that happened to us once. We borrowed a movie from a friend and popped it in the DVD player. The scene opened in the perfect place to make it seem like it was the start of the film. But the characters and their relationships made no sense at all. The setting was so strange and it felt like we'd missed something critical. Then suddenly, after about 45 minutes of watching this crazy movie, it ended. We were so confused. Until we checked the film length on the back of the case and realized we missed the entire first hour. So we started from the beginning and boy, did the story make a whole lot more sense now.

The Bible needs to be read in context because the whole book tells the whole story.

Yes, each individual book in the Bible (like Genesis, Isaiah, Matthew, Galatians), can be read from start to finish, but really it is like watching one scene from a movie — kind of like going to watch a YouTube clip from your favorite film. If you know the whole movie, that clip makes so much sense. If you're showing it to someone who doesn't know the

54

movie at all, you'll have to set up the clip in order for it to make sense, right?

So my point is this: You won't be able to really know God's truth apart from Satan's lies if you don't read your Bible to learn it for yourself. Of course, you'll also need the input and guidance of an older Christian — like a pastor, youth leader, mentor, or parent — to help you put the pieces together until you get through reading the whole Bible on your own over a number of years.

Searching for the Truth

Uncovering our true identity in Christ is about determinedly stepping out of a false belief system — stinkin' thinkin' — and into the truth. It requires being aware of every thought and putting it up against the test of Scripture. That's exactly what these two verses tell us to do:

> *2 Corinthians 10:5*
> *We demolish arguments and every pretension that sets itself up against the knowledge of God, and we take captive every thought to make it obedient to Christ.*

> *Romans 12:2*
> *Do not conform any longer to the pattern of this world, but be transformed by the renewing of your mind.*

Taking captive false beliefs and replacing them with the truth is a life skill and discipline, where we choose to embrace God's truth over what we feel or think is truth. It is like a distance runner choosing a new course, even though the old one felt just fine. On the new course, the runners have to pay attention to the terrain in order to make sure they don't stumble and fall. They will need to know when and where they'll have to pace themselves so that the uphill climbs won't wear them down.

Developing a new thinking pattern is a matter of practice and determination. It takes the ability to recognize the lies we believe along

WORTH WATCHING

As you prepare to lead your girls through this chapter, I highly recommend taking the time to listen or watch a fantastic sermon by Pastor Brad Bigney, "Are Christians Really Dead to Sin?".

While this sermon picks up in the middle of a series on Romans, Pastor Bigney talks about what we believe and how we need to live by the Truth and not our feelings. You'll be encouraged, for sure!

You can find the sermon here: https://graceky.org/sermons/ message/18-are-christians-real-ly-dead-to-sin/watch

CHECK the PULSE

How do you see the girls processing this information?

Are they discovering that their feelings and the Truth are not necessarily the same?

If the girls did not do this part of the chapter at home, take time to have them work on it during the session.

If you need a printable copy, you can find one at moretobe.com/freedom-resources.

with the truths we need to embrace, and that comes through studying Scripture and the counsel of Christian mentors and parents.

For example, you might have a thought like this:

I feel so alone today.

But that thought needs to be captured and put in the context of truth, like this:

Yes, right now, right here I am alone, without another person, but I am never totally alone because I belong to God (1 Peter 2:9) and He is always with me (Deut. 31:6-8).

Of course, how do you know what a lie is in the first place? And how do you know where to find the Scripture truth, especially if you don't know how to study your Bible? Well, read on and you'll begin to see some of the core lies we all face and the truths we can use to overcome them.

What do you believe?

So do you know how to find out if your beliefs are based on truth? How about we take a little quiz? Don't worry, you won't be graded! Read through the list of statements below and mark each one as follows:

A = **Always. . . this is the way I always feel**
S = **Sometimes. . . this is the way I sometimes feel**
N = **Never. . . this is never the way I feel**

_____ If it feels right, then it must be right.

_____ I can only feel good about myself if I do it perfectly.

_____ If I can't win, why bother?

_____ I hate it when everyone isn't happy with me.

_____ I am the way I am.

_____ Things never work out for me.

_____ Life should be easy, or I must be doing something wrong.

_____ I won't be happy unless they do it my way.

_____ I know it is always my fault when things go wrong.

_____ Why doesn't anyone ever consider me?

_____ People never thank me for what I do for them.

_____ A person should have it all, no matter what.

_____ I don't think you should have to wait for what you want.

_____ Relationships shouldn't be hard if they are meant to be.

_____ How well I do something determines how good I feel about myself.

_____ I believe that people are basically good.

_____ If it is hard, I should quit.

_____ It is so hard to trust anyone.

_____ If am I good enough, God will protect me from getting hurt.

_____ God doesn't have time for my problems.

_____ A good Christian doesn't get angry, anxious, or depressed.

Now it's time to total your answers. What was your result?

_____ # of A = Always

57

_____ # of S = Sometimes

_____ # of N =Never

Can you guess how you're doing on believing lies versus the truth? Well, every one of those statements reflects a core lie. That means, for any that you marked with an A or S reflects thinking that is inconsistent with Biblical truth. Don't despair! Remember, there is no way for you to know the truth if you don't study the Scriptures. That's why we're going through this study! Like a runner in a race, we need to press on to the next mile, even if we'd like a break about now. Let's continue to look at Biblical truths so that we can demolish the lies we believe.

The Real Truth

Below you'll see of statements that include the core lie, the Biblical truth, and the verses where that truth is found.

Lie: I must be perfect.
TRUTH: Christ is perfect.
Verses: Rom 3:22-23, 1 John 1:8, Psalm 18:30, Phil 3:12, Matt 4:8

Lie: I must have everyone's love and approval.
TRUTH: I am approved by God.
Verses: Col 3:23-24; Gal 1:10

Lie: It is easier to avoid problems than to face them.
TRUTH: God promises that this life will have problems.
Verses: Phil 3:13-14

Lie: You can have it all.
TRUTH: A yes is always a no, and a no always a yes.

Verses:	1 John 2:15-17

Lie:	My worth is determined by my performance.
TRUTH:	Your worth is found in Whose you are.
Verses:	Psalm 139:13-14; Romans 12:3

Lie:	Life should be easy.
TRUTH:	We are promised trouble in this world.
Verses:	John 16:33, Matt 6:34

Lie:	You shouldn't have to wait for what you want.
TRUTH:	Waiting is always part of life.
Verses:	Gal 6:7-8; Pro 14:29

Lie:	People are basically good.
TRUTH:	No one is good. Not one.
Verses:	Jer 17:9; Matt 15:19; Rom 3:10-12; Gal 5:19-21

Lie:	This relationship is hard, therefore it must be wrong.
TRUTH:	Relationships are hard and we are to work together to resolve challenges.
Verses:	1 Cor 7:28 (marriage), Heb 12:14

Lie:	God's love must be earned.
TRUTH:	God's love is free and unconditional.
Verses:	Rom 5:8; Eph 2:8-9; John 3:16

Lie:	Because I am a Christian, God will protect me from suffering.
TRUTH:	God allows us to experience suffering, trials, and pain.
Verses:	1 Pet 4:12-13, John 16:33; Phil 1:29

Lie:	A good Christian doesn't feel angry, depressed, or anxious.
TRUTH:	We are emotional beings held accountable for our actions but sometimes we need professional help to work through our emotions.
Verses:	John 11:33-35; Mark 14:32-34; Mark 11:15-16

ACTIVITY TIME

If just reading through these lies versus truths seems a little too boring for your girls, how about doing a skit or a game?

Skit Time

- Pick one of the lies and on an index card, write down a scenario to illustrate a time in which that type of lie plays out.

- Include the names of two characters, a likely setting, and a conflict situation.

- Have two of the girls act it out and ask the other girls to guess the lie.

- Challenge the girls to role play how the Truth could change the scene.

--> continued on next page

Lie:	This always happens to me.
TRUTH:	What a person does to you is more a reflection of them than you.
Verses:	Mathew 12:34; Luke 6:45

Lie:	If I feel it, then it must be true.
TRUTH:	Truth is not based on feelings but fact. All truth is God's truth.
Verses:	John 17:17

Can you believe this isn't even a complete list? Well, it's not. There are many more lies we believe! But this is a good starting place.

Your Turn

Can you see how important is it to pay attention to what you believe in light of what the Scripture says is true? I hope so, because in order to run this spiritual race with the stamina you'll need to finish well, you'll need to know the truth. You'll need to make the decision to practice taking captive your thoughts and making sure they line up with the truth. As you move into this habit, consider these important steps:

1. *Let the Spirit Guide You*

When you put your faith in Jesus, God promises to give us the Holy Spirit to lead and guide us. The Spirit draws upon the Word and prompts you how to live, reminding you of the truth. But you can easily "shush" up the Spirit if you turn to your old belief patterns and habits. Instead, spend time reading your Bible so that you can learn what God says is true. (Psalm 37:4, Proverbs 4:23, Psalm 147:3)

2. *Be Careful of Influences*

You will be bombarded by messages from this world as well as through your relationships with friends and teachers. Be aware of the thinking and philosophy of those around you, as well as the messages being conveyed through the media. These things will significantly influence your thinking and may entice you to make decisions contrary to God's word. (Romans 12:2, 2 Corinthians 10:13)

3. *Know Your Own Flesh*

Knowing your flesh is about being aware of the ways you are easily tempted to disobey God's word. Your flesh will respond to anything that looks exciting and that promises to satisfy your longing for significance. Satan plays on your fleshly desires, tempting you with lies to do what is contrary to the Holy Spirit's leading, so be sure to have accountability partners in place to help you! (Mark 14:38, 2 Timothy 2:22, 1 Corinthians 10:23, Matthew 5:14)

4. *Listen to your Heart and Your Mouth*

Did you know that what comes out of your mouth reveals what you think and feel? Scripture says, out of the heart the mouth speaks. So that means you can learn about what you believe based on what you say! Listen to your heart and mouth, and deal honestly with God so that you will be free to respond to the Holy Spirit's leading and be quick to obey God's Word. (Matthew 12:34)

When you begin to live out of a place of truth, your life will be transformed from the inside out.

Your identity will no longer be defined by how you feel, but by who you are — God's holy child — set apart for His good purposes.

Game Time

- Write out the lies on one set of index cards in red and the truths out on another set in green.

- Tape the cards to a wall, where all the girls can see them.

- Create two teams and tell the girls the goal is to find the most matches of lies and truths.

- Set a timer for less than five minutes and see what they get. In order to win the match, each team can use a whistle, bell, or tambourine for them to rattle in order to claim their match.

- Each set counts as five points. For a tie-breaker, see if the girls can recall the Bible verse that matches the Truth.

61

Those feelings of guilt or shame, hurt or frustration, insecurity or being overlooked may still rise up in you, but now you'll have a way of fighting back. With God's Word as your guide, your identity will win over your swaying feelings.

> *God, thank You so much for giving us Your Truth to live by. The Bible really is more than a guidebook or set of rules. It is Your love letter to us, reminding us of who we are and how we are to live in a way that brings joy, blessing, and purpose to our lives. Please help us, God, to be able to understand Your Word. Bring us teachers, who love You and know Your truth, so that they can teach us and encourage us. Give us wisdom beyond our years, so that we can live according to Your Truth without compromise. In Jesus' Name, Amen.*

*The beliefs quiz was inspired by Dr. Chris Thurman and the concepts he presents in his book, *The Lies We Believe.*

Time to Stretch Questions

1. What major life circumstances, experiences, or relationships have shaped your beliefs, both in terms of those that fall into the "core lies" category and those that reflect God's truths?

A PLAN TO STRETCH
Which option will work for you this week?

Option 1 -
Bible Study Format
• discuss the questions
• use index cards to help with sharing

Option 2 -
Mentoring Gathering Format
• download the questions from moretobe.com/freedom-resources
• send home with the girls

Option 3 -
Time Sensitive Needs
• send home the questions
• discuss in the next session

BRAINSTORM

Make time to discuss with your girls the ways they can go about developing new habits built on truth.

The oneDEGREE resource will provide with practical ideas and principles to support this process. You can find it here: moretobe.com/onedegree-de-termining-your-life-course/

2. As you look at the results of your beliefs quiz, which two or three lies are most troubling to you — or surprise you? Would you be willing to pray about those right now and discuss them with your mom or mentor?

3. What top three truths from the "truths list" do you feel God wants you to concentrate on embracing personally? Write down those key verses below and journal a bit about why you think these matter so much.

4. Can you think of certain statements or beliefs that you finding yourself saying, which weren't in the list, that might be inconsistent with Scripture? Write those down and seek out an older Christian to help you search the Bible to find the counter-truth.

EXTRA HELP

Is praying something that you know you ought to do but find it to be a struggle? Do you squirm when it is time to pray out loud? Do you sometimes feel at a loss to know how to pray for others, especially during difficult times? Well, you're not alone!

Praying is a challenge for many Christians. Let me encourage you to download the "How to Open Up to God" resource for encouragement and practical ideas: moretobe.com/2012/03/20/download-prayer-ideas-for-opening-up-to-god/

5. Read Romans 12:2 and 2 Corinthians 10:5 below, and then write out those Scriptures in the form of a prayer. Ask God to teach you how to believe His Word so that His Truth shapes your identity.

Romans 12:2 NIV
Do not conform to the pattern of this world, but be transformed by the renewing of your mind. Then you will be able to test and approve what God's will is—his good, pleasing and perfect will.

2 Corinthians 10:5 NIV
We demolish arguments and every pretension that sets itself up against the knowledge of God, and we take captive every thought to make it obedient to Christ.

Visit http://www.moretobe.com/freedom-resources for chapter-by-chapter resources and links.

CHAPTER FOUR

Embracing Your Place

Romans 12:3-5 NIV
. . . For just as each of us has one body with many members,
and these members do not all have the same function,
so in Christ we, though many, form one body,
and each member belongs to all the others.

Even though I have "Member of the Track Team" included on my list of high school accomplishments, it's not exactly something I look back on with great excitement. Track wasn't my passion. It was the last resort, and the only way I could continue to be an athlete within the limitations of my own body. Dance was over, soccer was out of the question, and I quit cheerleading out of self-respect. (I'm sorry, but crawling on the gym floor towards the football team during pep rally as a part of our dance-cheer routine was not my idea of being a strong, respectable young woman. So yeah, I quit that very day.)

Each day, I'd show up to practice on time with my gear on, but I only half-heartedly wanting to be there. Sure, I wanted to win my race, but I dreaded the warm ups and conditioning exercises. I was so darn slow, and always winded, which made me feel a bit like a loser every single day. I was one insignificant girl on a team I didn't feel connected to, but was committed to fulfilling this one last requirement before graduating and moving on with the rest of my life.

67

GET READY CHECKLIST

One Week Ahead of Time
- Spend time in prayer and doing the study for yourself.
- Pick activities to do.
- Shop for any supplies.
- Consider picking up a treat.
- Make sure you have enough tea, cups, sugar, and milk.
- Send a text or email reminder the day before.

Meeting Time
- Have on hand Bibles along with extra pens and pencils.
- Don't forget to boil the water.
- You're at the finish line. . . press hard to the end for the glory of God!

It's interesting to me how my track experience paints such an accurate picture of my real life. Sometimes, we find ourselves in situations and relationships where we feel out of place, unqualified, insignificant, and overlooked.

We may have to do things that we're not passionate about.

We may feel unqualified, yet have to fill a position or meet a need.

We may think the responsibilities are pointless and not a whole lot of fun.

We may wish we were doing something else where we can be noticed and appreciated.

We may feel this way for a day, a week, a month, or a year. Depending on our circumstances and relationships, we may wonder,

"God, why am I here? What is it that you want to do in my life? Does this have to go on this way?"

Trust me. Most days I showed up to track practice feeling nothing but sadness. After 13 years of dancing, with up to three hours a day invested three days a week, I had nothing to show for it. Just memories and lost dreams. I was the youngest to go on pointe in my class and was about to join the competitive dance team — a dream I had from the time I was little. But instead, I had a freak accident that wrecked my knee. At the time, we thought it was just a little dislocation and with a brace, I'd be back to normal after it healed. But then it happened again a few months later. And again. I recovered and quickly learned all my dance routines in time for the recital, only to dislocate it the week before. I was done. No matter how much I wanted to continue, my body had other plans and my life course was re-routed.

When Our Course is Re-routed

I'm certainly not alone in this experience of having a dream dashed.

68

Living at a boarding and day college prep school for the last 17 years has given me a broader perspective on how often we're called to surrender our dreams and give up our passions, even as teens. I can think of a dozen athletes that were destined for college scholarships, and some even got them, who suffered an unlikely injury at the worst time. It turned their competitive course in a new direction, while stripping away their dreams and sometimes their identity, too.

Whether you're an athlete or a musician, the class president or a servant leader, the girl with a dozen best friends you've known since preschool or one super close friend you've made since moving to your new hometown, you've likely been in a situation where you've defined yourself by your accomplishments and dreams. . . and then suddenly *that one thing* is no longer is a part of your life.

You know that feeling of being crushed. You know how naked it feels to walk out of your home, without the comfort of your identity rooted in what you do. You know what it feels like to be the one who is overlooked because you can no longer contribute the way you once did.

> ***The process of surrender is the ripping away of what you want — or who you thought you were — and allowing God to accomplish His purposes in you and through you in a different way.***

Oh, surrender hurts! But we must grieve the loss and embrace the new beginning. We can shed a few messy tears on our parent's shoulders — and we definitely should, because keeping our feelings all stuffed away isn't healthy. And we can cry out to God, telling Him about our disappointments. He can handle our temper tantrums. Look at the Psalms. They are filled with fits of disappointment, giving us permission to be honest with God. And yet the Psalmist moves from sadness to embracing God's purposes. How? By forming new thoughts in line with God's character and eternal purpose.

> *Psalm 42:5 NIV*
> *Why, my soul, are you downcast?*

INSPIRING STORIES

The stories of broken dreams turned into unexpected blessings are too many to count. . . and are often forgotten. These two stories capture the message of this chapter with sincerity and transparency.

- Paralympian Stef Reid talks about the boating accident that changed her life. http://fervr.net/videos/i-lost-my-leg-but-found-my-god

- A story about a young woman and her broken dream http://cvcnow.com/portfolio/my-broken-dream/

If you have a story to share, think about how you can communicate in a way that gives God the glory and reveals His faithfulness. Be sure to share about the process you had to go through to get to the other side of grief into receiving God's blessing.

Why so disturbed within me?
Put your hope in God,
for I will yet praise him,
my Savior and my God.

The Psalmist is honest, admitting his downcast feelings, but in the same breath turns his mind to remember the truth — that he can put his hope in God. Throughout the Psalms, we see reminders of God's faithfulness, provisions, and plans, even in the midst of difficult circumstances. When we take our thoughts captive and replace them with God's truth, like the Psalmist, then we position ourselves to see the new thing God is doing in our lives. This is the exact moment in which God takes us from a place of despair to a place of hope — where we can see new opportunities. This is how we can begin seeing our significance in light of God's new purposes for our lives.

> ***Overlooked and disappointed isn't***
> ***where you or I are meant to live.***

God intended better than that for each one of us, but it requires a willingness on our part to embrace the race — our life race — even as the course changes. How do we do that? By defining ourselves according to our identity in Christ instead of by what we accomplish or who we are connected, too.

Being a Part of Something Bigger

Have you ever noticed that when you're a part of something — like a team, club, or program — it gives you a sense of belonging and worth. When we are forced off a team because of an injury, or out of a community because our family has to move, we're left feeling both alone and overlooked.

> ***Until we find our place to belong,***
> ***there will always be an emptiness inside of us.***

70

Well, that's not really a bad thing, because God did design us to need each other — but more importantly than needing a club or a team, God wants us to be connected with the body of Christ. In the Bible, God describes the family of God as the Body of Christ, and compares the many parts in His family with the many parts that make up our own physical body. Take a minute to read carefully how God describes the significance of our part in the body of Christ.

1 Corinthians 12:12-31 MSG

You can easily enough see how this kind of thing works by looking no further than your own body. Your body has many parts—limbs, organs, cells—but no matter how many parts you can name, you're still one body. It's exactly the same with Christ. By means of his one Spirit, we all said good-bye to our partial and piecemeal lives. We each used to independently call our own shots, but then we entered into a large and integrated life in which he has the final say in everything. . .

I want you to think about how all this makes you more significant, not less. A body isn't just a single part blown up into something huge. It's all the different-but-similar parts arranged and functioning together. If Foot said, "I'm not elegant like Hand, embellished with rings; I guess I don't belong to this body," would that make it so? If Ear said, "I'm not beautiful like Eye, limpid and expressive; I don't deserve a place on the head," would you want to remove it from the body? If the body was all eye, how could it hear? If all ear, how could it smell? As it is, we see that God has carefully placed each part of the body right where he wanted it.

But I also want you to think about how this keeps your significance from getting blown up into self-importance. For no matter how significant you are, it is only because of what you are a part of.

An enormous eye or a gigantic hand wouldn't be a body, but a monster. What we have is one body with many parts, each its proper size and in its proper place. No part is important on its own. Can you imagine Eye telling Hand, "Get lost; I don't need you"? Or, Head telling Foot, "You're fired; your job has been phased out"? As a matter of fact, in practice it works the

71

STOP & SHARE

Have you been able to recognize your part in the body of Christ? Do you see the way God is using your gifts and talents?

If so, take the time to share with the girls about your part in the body of Christ and the way it meets a need to belong.

If the idea of belonging to the body of Christ is something you've yet to experience for yourself, spend time in prayer and ask God to show you where and when you can plug in. Be brave and reach out to your pastor or women's ministry leader for their perspective and direction.

You may also want to use some of the resources available at elisapulliam.com and consider life coaching as a way to discover your God-given place in the body of Christ.

other way—the "lower" the part, the more basic, and therefore necessary. You can live without an eye, for instance, but not without a stomach. When it's a part of your own body you are concerned with, it makes no difference whether the part is visible or clothed, higher or lower. You give it dignity and honor just as it is, without comparisons. If anything, you have more concern for the lower parts than the higher. If you had to choose, wouldn't you prefer good digestion to full-bodied hair?

The way God designed our bodies is a model for understanding our lives together as a church: every part dependent on every other part, the parts we mention and the parts we don't, the parts we see and the parts we don't. If one part hurts, every other part is involved in the hurt, and in the healing. If one part flourishes, every other part enters into the exuberance.

Can't you see how God desperately wants you to move into a complete understanding of your significance as you find your place in the body of Christ?

Your part in the family of God is priceless.

Your part is necessary and valuable, but it's not dependent on how good you are, how much you can do, or when you exceed everyone's wildest expectations. Your part is based on how God has made you and the way in which you can serve as you surrender your life to Him.

If you read further along in 1 Corinthians 12, you'll see that God appoints each person with a different gift — a different way of participating in the family of God. These gifts aren't exactly like a job, where you show up with skills and qualifications. You don't get trained in order to get your gifts either. The spiritual gifts are given by God for His purposes. They are designed to meet the needs within the family of God, but also can bless and serve those who've yet to know Him. The list of gifts are kind of unusual, too, as they aren't things we get to open up but are rather something we become — like apostles, prophets, teachers, miracle workers, healers, helpers, organizers, those who pray in tongues. But before you panic about what these gifts mean and which one you may have, keep this in mind:

Figuring out the gift God has put inside of you may be impossible because you've yet to experience enough life to recognize the way God intends to use you in the family of God.

So rather than looking at the list of gifts and wondering which one is yours, remind yourself of this perspective:

"Well, I don't know what gift God has given me, but I know He's promised to give each one of us a gift to use in the body of Christ, so I'll just keep looking for ways to connect and serve the body until I discover which one is mine."

Your spiritual gift is only a clue pointing to your life purpose. God has also put together your personality, skills, and talents. He's orchestrated your experiences, family, and friendships. All of these things come together to both reveal your life purpose and the ways God wants to use you on this earth.

One day you'll see what God is up to. As you embrace this race — your life race — you'll discover your significance is based on the way God uniquely designed you to fit into His family, and to draw others into His family. Then you'll realize that what you do and how you do it isn't as important as where He's put you and how He's made you to live. If you live surrendered to His plans, you'll have no regrets.

How Do You Embrace Your Place?

So how exactly do you embrace your place in God's family when you don't really know what you've been made to do? There's no perfect formula, but there are steps you can take to move forward. Like building blocks, you can work through the process of embracing your identity in Christ while learning how to take captive your thoughts to make them line up with God's truth. As you get comfortable living that way, you can add on these steps:

73

1. *Watch Out for the Rejection Stamp*

The hurt that comes from feeling insignificant and overlooked stems from a desire to belong to something greater than ourselves. The trouble really comes when the great big rejection stamp pounds down on our lives with a simple little lie from the Enemy imprinted in our soul: You don't matter to anyone, not now, not ever. Nothing could be further from the truth! You matter first and foremost to God. He created you and designed you for a unique purpose. When Satan's condemning thoughts wrestle out the truth, an imprint is left in your heart and mind, reshaping your identity and rerouting your calling. This is why you must guard your thoughts, so that only the Truth will impact your soul and the rejection stamp will leave no mark on you. (John 8:44, 2 Corinthians 10:5)

2. *Get With a Godly Friend or Family Member and Pray!*

Sometimes the best help in moving out of a place of feeling insignificant is through having a friend, mentor, or family member encourage you through the hard times. When you're stuck in a place of feeling defeated, reach out to another Christian to confess your feelings and pray together. God uses prayer as a way to heal our hurting hearts, so turn to Him with the help of someone you can trust. (James 5:16, Romans 8:26, 12:12; Ephesians 1:16-18, 3:16-20)

3. *Reach Out, Reach Beyond*

When your focus becomes about me, myself, and I, you'll end up feeling more and more sad and worthless. So make the decision to reach out to others and reach beyond your circumstances, even before you feel like doing so. If you've brought your disappointments to God and spent time in prayer, with a trusted mentor or parent, then make the decision to step out in faith as you embrace the new race before you.

AS GOES THE MENTOR

Do you have a godly friend or mentor you can pray with on a regular basis? If not, let me suggest these possibilities:

- Consider the women your age and older at your church, but don't limit yourself to only your friends. Acquaintances are certainly possibilities for creating prayer partnerships.

- Are there younger women who might like to have you as their prayer partner? Consider younger moms or youth leaders who might like to connect with you for prayer, too.

If you'd like to consider more on cultivating a mentoring relationship, read "Impact My Life: Biblical Mentoring Simplified," which is available on Amazon.

Maybe you can even reach others who feel overlooked or insignificant. The Bible tells us that God wants us to comfort others, especially after we've been comforted by Him:

2 Corinthians 1:3-5 MSG
He comes alongside us when we go through hard times, and before you know it, he brings us alongside someone else who is going through hard times so that we can be there for that person just as God was there for us.

So is God asking you to reach out to someone who is experiencing what you've experienced?

God has a purpose for your life, friend. Even if you feel like it's been thrown off the side of a cliff, it doesn't mean you're going to come crashing to the ground.

> ***Maybe God's plans for you include a wildly magnificent rescue, where He swoops in, catches you in the palm of His hands, and transports you to an entirely new place. He fills your life with amazing new opportunities — ones you you would have never known if the course stayed the same.***

So will you let Him direct your steps as you run the race He's marked out for you?

The Journey to Freedom Begins

Do you see the finish line of this study right in front you? Well, here we are. . . all done except for a few remaining questions. You've made it through four full chapters of information, and hopefully, you now have a brand new understanding of what it means to be a child of God. You've gained a new perspective about how to figure out if what you feel is actually true, and how to kick those annoying lies to curb. And, you've been given the opportunity to think about how to respond to life's disappointments while also finding purpose by being a perfectly unique and needed member in the family of God.

75

Can you believe that in such a short time you've been given so much information to use on this life journey — this journey of freedom!

John 8:32 NIV
Then you will know the truth, and the truth will set you free.

Now you can decide for yourself what you want to believe. You can make wise decisions about how you want to live. You can find joy in embracing your God-given purposes on this earth!

So are you ready to run — to press on — and finish the race before you?

Are you ready to share with the world about how you've discovered your identity in Christ?

Girls, if it is the journey to freedom you want, then embrace what God says about you. It is His opinion that matters most. In His truth your freedom is found.

Heavenly Father, it is so hard to not know Your plans for our lives. When things go off course and we find ourselves losing our dreams, we just want to crumble up in a pity party of tears. But God, please comfort us in this moment. Show us that there is more to life than what we think we wanted or feel we needed. Show us, Lord, the ways you're working in us and through us, even in an unlikely situation. Help us to surrender our plans to You. Help us to embrace this race you've set out for us to run, and find delight in fulfilling your purposes. In Jesus' Name, Amen.

Time to Stretch Questions

1. Have you faced a situation or circumstance, which left you feeling overlooked, insignificant, or disappointed? Take some time to consider how you felt and what you learned from that situation or experience. But don't stop there. Also consider what God might have to say about it. Record your thoughts below.

A PLAN TO STRETCH
Which option will work for you this week?

Option 1 -
Bible Study Format
- discuss the questions
- use index cards to help with sharing

Option 2 -
Mentoring Gathering Format
- download the questions from moretobe.com/freedom-resources
- send home with the girls

Option 3 -
Time Sensitive Needs
- send home the questions
- discuss in the next session

STOP & SHARE

If you've not already shared a story about how God has redirected your life course, consider doing so now. Think about painting the picture of God's faithfulness to you in times like:

- Moving with your family and making new friends.
- Having to give up your dream because of an illness, injury, or even financial pressure on your family.
- Deciding on a different college, job, or ministry because of a change in plans or expectations.
- How your plans to get married and have children didn't match God's plans.

As you frame your story, keep the focus on glorifying God — or as I heard a pastor once say, "Make God bigger!" Feel free to use humor and transparency to help connect with the girls, too.

2. When you look back on your life, can you see times in which God has redirected your life course? Looking at it from this perspective, can you see His purposes or are you still wondering? What Bible verse might capture what God is doing in you or through you as it relates to this experience?

3. What are your thoughts about God's faithfulness? Do you think He'll come through for you or leave you disappointed? Do you trust Him to meet your needs and love you unconditionally? Share how you really feel and also ask God to give you His perspective.

4. Take about 10 minutes to search for the word "faithful" and "faithfulness" on Biblegateway.com. Skim through the verses and write down three that stand out to you. Commit to memorizing these verses so that you can quote them when you need to remember about God's faithfulness in the future.

5. We've talked about the significant part you get play in the family of God. How does knowing this truth make you feel? Can you see yourself functioning in that way now?

6. Take a few minutes to read the passage from Romans below, which reminds us about our part in the body of Christ. Then use the prayer prompts to talk with the Lord about your life, identity, and purpose in the family of God.

    Romans 12:3-5 NIV
    For by the grace given me I say to every one of you: Do not think of your-self more highly than you ought, but rather think of yourself with sober judgment, in accordance with the faith God has distributed to each of you. For just as each of us has one body with many members, and these members do not all have the same function, so in Christ we, though many, form one body, and each member belongs to all the others.

God, as I come before you today, I am sure I have thought of myself as more highly than I ought. Please forgive me for feeling this way. . .

God, I ask you to help me, teach me how to think of myself with sober judgment {without pride or arrogance} and show me the areas in which I can be prideful, critical, arrogant, self-serving. . .

God, you have given me the gift of faith. Help me to walk in faith and give up my need to control my life and others. . .

USING PRAYER PROMPTS

Using Scripture as a framework for praying is foreign for many of us, but really, it should be our primary guide and focus.

If God already tells us what is true and what to be careful about in the Bible, why not use the Word to open our hearts and minds to the will of Heavenly Father during our times of prayer?

If the girls struggle in this process, take the time to help them through it in your time together.

God you promise that I am significant because I am part of your family and designed to meet a need in the body of Christ. Please show me the ways You want to use me to serve. . .

my family . . .

my friends . . .

my school . . .

my work . . .

I know, God, that I long to belong. Please show me where I ought to be careful, so that I don't pursue belonging to the wrong crowd or chase after the wrong opportunity. . .

82

Lord, help me to focus on having this need met within the body of Christ, with these people. . . .

Make me, Lord, to be willing to meet their needs, and not just my own, as I remember my purpose within Your family and find my identity rooted in what you have to say about me. . .

In Jesus' Name, Amen.

IT'S A WRAP

Congratulations for making it to the end of this study with your girls. It's been quite a journey, I'm sure.

As you wrap up your last session, consider ways to celebrate and leave a "stone of remembrance" to mark this accomplishment, such as:

- Plan a party with a special theme.
- Enter into a 5K type of race together as a team.
- Make a piece of jewelry to help remember the lessons.

Be creative and unique as you give glory to God for this great accomplishment.

**Visit http://www.moretobe.com/freedom-resources
for chapter-by-chapter resources and links.**

CONCLUSION

Before You Close the Book

In the same way I had you start with dedicating this study to the Lord,
I want to give you a challenge to finish it with Him, too.

Use the prompts below to record your thoughts and prayers.

God, I want to close this study thanking you for. . .

I can see now how you used this study to teach me. . .

As I look at the way I served, I am glad that I. . .

Next time I serve this way, I want to remember. . .

I am trusting these girls into your care. . .

Acknowledgements

Sometimes it takes a NO to show you another YES. And that, my friends, is how this study took shape. In the face of an apparent dead-end, I turned to the Lord and pleaded with Him, "What now?"

For weeks, maybe even months, I heard nothing. Well, not nothing, but rather the reminder to be focused on living from the overflow of Christ in my life, serving those right in my home, my community, and my little plot on this earth. And it was in the serving that I remembered where my passions were rooted and my ministry began. It was in doing real life that I could see there were needs God designed me to meet, even if they weren't what I expected.

And so, as I look at this study, I remember the people who God used to make me see His purposes and carry them out. . .

Girls next door, thank you for letting me share my story and for your amazing questions that reminded me there was a need I could meet.

Girls across the field, thank you for your innocent request that I should write a book and reminding me that my motherly words mean much to you.

My own girls, thank you for the research you put in and the cheering from the sidelines as I hauled away to write.

My dear twinables, thank you for being patient, waiting on mommy to be done and being proud of how my time was spent.

My amazing husband, who reminds me I can and should write, but first I should serve-in-the-flesh and remember my own boundary-keeping priorities.

My dear SBS sisters, your fellowship on the hope retreat nurtured my soul and I am certain your prayers in the weeks to follow were used by God to give life to this study.

My wonderful team at *More to Be*, you never cease to amaze me with your willingness to join in my crazy ideas and help me carry them out with gusto. And a special thanks to Christine, Suz, and Paige for their thoughtful and careful proofreading of this study.

And to the Lord, who made me for His purposes, constantly transforming me from the inside out and being willing to use me in my mess for His glory. This is for You. Because You made me love this generation of girls so much.

About the Author

Elisa Pulliam, who prefers to be called Lisa, is a lifelong mentor, ministry leader, speaker and life coach, passionate about encouraging and equipping this generation of women to impact the next generation with relevant Truth.

After more than a decade of mothering and over fifteen years of mentoring teen girls coinciding with leading women's ministries, Elisa is in tune with the struggles of teens, twenty-somethings and today's women. Having lived a life apart from God, marked by a legacy of dysfunction and a long season of rebellion, Elisa understands the power of the Cross. When she met Jesus as her Lord and Savior during her junior year in college, her life radically changed, and her life calling soon emerged.

Elisa's deepest desire is to facilitate life transformation in others by offering practical, easily accessible, and biblically sound resources to touch the heart, mind and soul. She shares her insights, teaching materials, and mentoring resources at *More to Be*, and offers life coaching through elisapulliam.com. You can also find her contributing monthly at MothersofDaughters.com and TheBetterMom.com.

Although her schedule is full, she is refueled by hosting regular ETC gatherings for teen girls, speaking at women's events as well as for groups of teenagers. Her goal is to make the most of their time through capturing biblical truths through storytelling, transparently sharing her personal experiences, and tossing in a good bit of humor as she unravels life lessons.

Elisa's counts it pure joy to be Stephen's wife, who is not only her best friend but has been Christ-with-skin-on to her for seventeen years of marriage. She also considers it a privilege to train up her four children (ages 8 through 14), and admits that they have taught her the most about love, affection and total forgiveness.

Ephesians 3:7
By God's grace and mighty power, I have been
given the privilege of serving him by spreading
this Good News.

About More to Be

*More to Be is dedicated to engaging the next generation
through equipping moms of tweens and teens with biblically relevant
resources and encouraging women to step into significant mentoring roles.*

Through providing simple, easily accessible online resources, *More to Be* is committed to speaking to the hearts of tween, teen and twenty-something girls, while also influencing today's moms to be the vessels of Truth in their daughter's lives and to see Christian women to step out in faith in answering the call to mentor the next generation of young women.

- Online mentoring training and studies courses encourage women to follow Christ distinctly so that they may mentor biblically. Built on principles captured by Elisa Pulliam in her book, *"Impact My Life: Biblical Mentoring Simplified,"* (available on Amazon), the courses incorporate life coaching concepts with discipleship principles to equip all women to mentor.

- ETC. Mentoring and Mugs & Mornings Mentoring, presents a unique mentoring concept providing a format and collection of resources designed to equip women to lead mentoring groups in their homes and community.

- Topics & Truth FREE downloadable lessons (really curriculum without the binding) and Dig Deep Guides, provide a quick but thorough look at relevant topics steeped in biblical truth.

- Life Coaching is available for especially for mentors and moms looking to develop leadership and life skills as they discover how to use their God-given gifts and talents in a variety of settings.

- The Blog is a daily landing place, full of encouragement, relevant Truth, informational articles, and interesting links for today's teens, twenty-somethings, mentors, and women.

At the heart of *More to Be* is a vision to see women (young and old) become more bright, more beautiful, more like Jesus as a personally relevant God enters their lives (2 Corinthians 3:16-18 MSG) through mentoring relationships and resources grounded in biblical truth. This is what it means to experience life transformed -- a life where there is more to be as we become more like Him and impact the world around us.

If you have any questions about *More to Be*, please email more@moretobe.com or visit www.moretobe.com.

2 Corinthians 3: MSG
. . . when God is personally present, a living
Spirit. . . Nothing between us and God, our
faces shining with the brightness of his face. And
so we are transfigured much like the Messiah,
our lives gradually becoming brighter and more
beautiful as God enters our lives and we become
like him.

Have you enjoyed the journey?

I'd love to hear from you!

elisa@moretobe.com

Spread the Word

We'd love for you to share about *More to Be* and our *Engage Teen Bible Study Collection* with others!

moretobe.com

facebook.com/moretobe

twitter.com/moretobe

pinterest.com/elisapulliam

Made in the USA
Lexington, KY
28 January 2015